LOVE OF MY LIFE

LOVE OF MY LIFE

SHARING THE SNAPSHOTS THAT SHAPED ME

THADDUES SMITH

J Merrill Publishing, Inc.
434 Hillpine Drive
Columbus, OH 43207
www.JMerrill.pub

Library of Congress Control Number: 2021922024
ISBN-13: 978-1-954414-27-3 (Paperback)
ISBN-13: 978-1-954414-26-6 (eBook)

Book Title: Love of My Life
Author: Thaddues Smith
Editing: Dennis E. Brown

CONTENTS

A WORD FROM THE EDITOR

Few who dare to write will ever accomplish what Ms. Smith has provided in this series of snapshots that she has held over her years as gems of joy and treasures of happiness.

There is no pretense in her story. There is no attempt to insert the flowery phrases that she has undoubtedly admired from the authors she had read in all her years. There is merely the hush of authenticity that blossoms from her candor as the images spill onto the page.

These pages unfold to reveal something rare and charming, to say nothing of the flavor and texture of life in another time and place, farther from here than mere miles can measure, but at a distance that can never be covered without these windows to the past. They are told with no other purpose than to give us the chance to remember or discover the kind of grass-root heritage of strength that needs to be reborn in all of us.

The author's images of life could have been part of the webbed background in Perle Buck's *The Good Earth* or John Stenberg's earthy novels. Such classics were born from encountering the kind of humble and unassuming families that populated this nation's landscape everywhere the eye could see.

The editing task here was very challenging because the real chore was to safeguard the flavor of each story. This was not only about a time and place that is now far removed from us, but we have a rare glimpse of life that was anchored in moral choices and the commitment to values that had formed their way of life.

The language of the common folk of those days in such western towns and countrysides did not bear the trademarks of the universities where already the distortions of reason were being planted into the minds that would influence the future. This author reminisces with a guilelessness that reflects the common speech of her childhood that was not encumbered by the growing academic preoccupation with "proper" English, but rather this account flows with the free expression of the common labor force of the day in which the accents of truth that the cast who populated that place and time in history have left for us to rediscover and revive.

May the snapshots of another day awaken us to seek a settledness within us that we, too, can pass on to those who follow us.

CHAPTER 1
HOME IS WHERE IT ALL STARTED

My family lived on the farm when I was just a young girl.

Of a mornin', we would have our breakfast at home beginnin' with only a half cup of coffee and a pretty good helpin' of honey and honeycomb. Then came the biscuits, eggs, and bacon.

And away we would go to Grandma's house just close down the road " where we could get another ½-cup of coffee, honey and honeycomb, bacon, egg, and biscuit. We knew just how to work Grandma and Grandpa let the little one get by with things.

To this day, I have a picture in my mind of Grandpa always fixin' his shoes whenever they needed it. This one early morning, he had his nails out and his shoe on the repair holder, as usual. I am going by, not paying attention to where I was going or what I was doin', so I knocked his nails all over the floor. He scolded me, and it hurt my feelings' But my mad spell only lasted as long as it took for me to make my way back down to their place.

We was about five miles out of Ada. My daddy would walk into town to work and then walk home in the evening. Now that's what you called a man who wanted to work, but then, of course, he had bought a hundred and ten acres, so he had to work to pay for the· place.

As time went by, daddy got enough money to get him a car. And we thought we was livin' "uptown."

My daddy's brother Tom lived in the city. He once told daddy he could get a job up there with him if he wanted to come up there. So, daddy said, "That sounds good to me!" And so off we went to Oklahoma City. Grandma and grandpa went with us, and] We all got settled in. Things was not all that bad; a lot of it was kind of good for us. There was a lot of great people, cars, and stores. You name it, and it was there.

We had found a good neighborhood to live in.   But there were problems. One day the lady next door hung her laundry sheets over the line. Well, someone wiped their big "'8il (8-cylinder oil) feet" on the clean clothes, so she thought it was Wanda and me But we told mother, "No, it was not us." But Mother took us in the house, and oh what a whipping we got! About a week later, we found out kids in the next block did it, but it was too late. We got punished for something we did not do.

One night we was having supper, and we heard a cracking and a popping, and down came the kitchen ceiling. So our supper ended before it started, but no one got hurt. What a mess it was.

Daddy called the landlord and told him what had happened, and He told daddy that he would have someone there tomorrow to get it fixed and clean up the stuff. So, the next morning they were there. It was all fixed up in a couple of days and looked very nice.

Our house was on the corner, and there was a grocery store on the other corner. My sister Wanda and I could walk to the store where we got a chance to win the "Guess What." They had a piece of candy and a small toy about six inches long with paper rolled around them. Winning really made our day.

One day, Uncle Lou and Aunt Minnie came up from Chickasaw to see us, and Uncle Lou went with us to the store. So, we got a "guess what," of course. While we was going back to the house, I was tellin' Uncle Lou there is always a toy and a piece of candy in these. Well, I opened mine, and there was candy but no toy. Boy, I was mad. I told Uncle Lou he is just an old "sheeter"r. When we got home, Uncle Lou was telling mother I was trying to tell him something, but he could not understand me. So, I told mother he was just an old sheeter. When Mother told Uncle Lou I was trying to say "cheater," he thought it was funny. So, he said I will go back to the store with you and see what you get this time. Well, when we got to the store, I told the little man he was just an old sheeter, and he said, "Well, baby, I will give you another one. And, of course, that made me happy.

CHAPTER 2

A SUNDAY TO REMEMBER

On Sunday, Daddy was off work, and all that week, we had planned to walk downtown, which was not that far. We got ready and was all excited because it was going to be a busy day. So here we are goin' down the sidewalk and there in front of us was a really large woman with the biggest butt I had ever seen. I said, "Daddy, look. I could ride on that!"

When daddy called my full name Thaddues Teen Keeling I knew I was in trouble. He said you had better never be that rude again. The woman didn't say a word but believe me; my daddy had enough to say for the both of them. That was the last time I ever made a remark like that. And you know what I have now? My own big butt! So don't never make fun of something like that, or it just might come home to you sooner or later.

CHAPTER 3

THE WEEKEND UNCLE LEONARD WILL ALWAYS REMEMBER

Aunt Arebell and Uncle Leonard lived in the city. . On the weekends, lots of time we got to go over to their house and spend time with them. Well, they came and got us on this particular Saturday to take us to the show. I had just had my fifth birthday, and Uncle Leonard said, "Don't say nothing, and you can still get in free." I was very little for my age. We got to the ticket window, and Uncle Leonard asked for two adults and one child.

Somehow, I heard myself saying< "Uncle Leonard, but I just had my birthday" And he said, "Oh, you did?" with a strange look on his face; and my answer, "yes, you remember, don't you? He paid for two adults and two children without saying a word and

We got our tickets went in and sat down. He said, "You didn't mind me very well." I told him, "I am sorry."

Before the movie started, there was a drawing for a bag of groceries, and guess what? They drew my number. I told Uncle Leonard, "this is what I got for being honest." And he couldn't help himself; he chuckled and agreed with me.

I was so happy. I could hardly wait to tell mother and daddy what I did, and my number was drawn.

CHAPTER 4
SAYING "GOODBYE"

Even though we didn't always talk about it, we all could see that Grandpa was sick and getting sicker. Finally, after about six months, he passed away, so we made our way back to Ada for his funeral. I will never forget how they had his body laid at Uncle Groover's and Aunt Salley's house. He looked so peaceful. I was only five, but I remember that as if it was yesterday. After the funeral, of course, we had to part from the others and go back home, so daddy could work. We had been off like a week.

CHAPTER 5
NOTHIN' BUT HARD TIMES

S omewhere in the middle of all this movin', getting' settled, and sayin' goodbyes, the war started; and from all the talk, things was getting' worse both where the fightin' was as well as at home. You could only get sugar and gas if you had the stamps. It was the same thing with tires for the car and nearly everything else. We all had the stamps

Aunt Arebell and Mother would go on the streetcar. You didn't have to use stamps to ride the streetcar, but you paid with tokens. They knew a place where they had bins full of small pieces of material they could get to make us dresses for almost nothing. You see, Wanda was in the first grade, and I was in kindergarten, and Mother wanted to make school dresses for us. So every day for three weeks, Aunt Arebell and Mother made the same trip to get the material strips. One night when daddy got home, mother showed him the pieces of material they had purchased. That's when daddy told mother, "You have all the material you need until you see if you can make them some dresses. Don't buy anymore 'til you can get some of that sewed up and see how it is going to look".

So, early the next morning, when Aunt Arebell got there, mother told her what Daddy had said. "Well, Lou, we better get busy and get to sewin'." And they got out the patterns and scissors and pins and started to work. By late afternoon, they had us two dresses, each made up. When we got home from school, mother fixed our hair up pretty; and when daddy got home from work, we was all set to show him how we looked and how pretty our new dresses was. He took one look and said, "Oh, how pretty! They fit perfect." He looked at mother and said, " Go get more material. You did a great job."

And, of course, that was just what they wanted him to say.

CHAPTER 6

THE NIGHT THE LIGHTS WENT OUT

And I remember the blackouts. The government has warned Oklahoma City that there was goin' to be blackouts. Sure enough, one day, when Daddy was at work, they turned out every light in Oklahoma City. He was on the top floor of the First National Bank and had no way down to the bottom.- He told Uncle Tom, "This is for the birds!"

Of course, Uncle Tom laughed, thinkin' it was funny. When the electricity came on, Daddy finished his job; and when he came home, he told Mother that we are packin' and goin' home. "I will let them know at the bank when I am leaving, and we are goin' home even if we all starve to death; because if they hit this town, we will be dead anyway. I wasn't sure who "they" were, but I was glad we weren't goin' to be there when it happened.

He got boxes, and mother and grandma started packin'. In two weeks, we was headed for the shack back home in Ada.

CHAPTER 7

COLD FEET – WARM HEARTS

This old house we lived in leaked like you would not believe. Mother would set a pan where the leaks was at to catch the water. She would always put a cloth in the pan, so that it didn't splash the water everywhere.

The cracks was so wide in the wall when it snowed, the snow would get on the foot of the bed. A many mornin' we would wake up with snow on our feet. But you know, we was a happy family. We was makin' it better than ever, but Daddy seemed to think we had to go to the cotton patch and pull cotton. Mother had fixed Wanda and myself a sack all our own to put our cotton in. We thought that was neat. All the money we made was ours to keep and buy whatever we wanted. But oh, it was cold out there.

Aunt Arebell went with us, but she didn't stay long. She told Daddy, "if you will take me to town, I will catch a bus and go home to Leonard and start complaining' about the cracks in the walls. And sure enough, that is what she did.

CHAPTER 8
THE BIG STORY ABOUT A BIG DOLL

There was this kid from Ada, and he found out our address. His name was Jackie Christian here comes a letter to me tellin' me he was gettin' me a big doll and sendin' it to me for Christmas. I just cried and cried. Mother said, "Oh, you will have to get him a present and send it to him for Christmas." I I didn't want to, but Mother said it was the right thing to do. So, when we went to town, and she got him a pair of toy guns to wear on his hips. And I cried again.

Well, it was like a week till Christmas, and here comes my box. It was sure not a big one. I opened it, and the cryin' was on again. He had got me a black doll with three braids on her head, but it was only about ten inches long. I was mad most of all because he had told a big story about the big doll he was sendin'; and then I get that thing. It hurt my feelings, but Mother made a big deal out of it.

Well, that has been like sixty-five years ago, and I still have the doll. Every time I go by it I think of Jackie.

It snowed so hard and much that you couldn't see the fence posts, and we begged daddy to take us home, so we could have Christmas at home. He told Mother, "Get packed, and let's go home." No heater in our car, so they heated bricks and put paper around them to keep our feet warm. We needed wood for the night once we were home, and the snow was so bad that Daddy wore one of our masks from Halloween to get wood, and we was ready to leave.

Daddy took us to town to buy whatever we wanted. We found a pair of white boots with white tassels on them. Man, we was steppin' high. We went down to show our neighbors which were black folks. And we told them that we was goin' home for Christmas and they both cried.

CHAPTER 9

MY OWN BROWN MULE

Every evening' when our work was done in the cotton fields and we was headed home, daddy would stop at the little store and he would ask what everyone wanted. This time I said oh daddy just get me a pop and a plug of Brown Mule chewin' tobacco. He took Mother's order and Wanda's too. When he came back, he handed me my pop and a plug of Brown Mule, gave Mother and Wanda what they had ordered, and we headed for the house.

I tore the paper from my Brown Mule and took a big chew. Let me tell you, the longer I chewed the worse it tasted. I asked Daddy if he would stop; I wanted to get read of that stuff. He said, "Why? You don't like it like you thought you would?" And I said "No, this is bad stuff." So, he pulled of the highway and I opened my door. I got rid of that pretty quick and washed my mouth out with some of my pop. Then Daddy handed me a candy bar. I took it, said "thanks" and I never again wanted no more tobacco of any kind.

CHAPTER 10
FEARS NOT FORGOTTEN

Every year we would go to Grandpa and Grandma East for Christmas Eve. That is when we would open our gifts. All our uncles and most of the cousins would get drunk. Wanda and I was afraid, but we was little and had to stay. Mother and Daddy knew that we was not goin' to get hurt. But we was still afraid.

And when summer came each year, Wanda and I wanted to go over and spend a few days with Grandma and Grandpa; so, Daddy would take us over there. They only lived about six miles from us. We was there about two days; and don't you know, it came up a cloud and looked like it was goin' to blow things away. Grandpa told Grandma to get things ready and let's go to the cellar. Wanda and I helped to open the door, and Grandpa said, "Get in there, kids!"

So here we are in a big hurry to get in the storm cellar and as I started in there was a big old black snake right over my head. Well, I begin to cry. I was afraid to go on in and Grandpa shouted "Get n in there. It's not goin' to hurt you. It's as afraid of you as you are of it." The cellar was old and made out of logs and finally that old snake went behind a big log. So, I went in slowly with Wanda behind me. Grandpa got in then Grandma came on in and closed the door. We lit a lamp, and I said "No tellin' how many more snakes is in this thing.". I was more afraid of snakes than I was the storm. We stayed in there about an hour, but it seemed much longer than that. And it was a happy time when we got out of there.

CHAPTER II

STILL ALIVE BUT NOT BY MUCH

Uncle Edd and Aunt Lela lived about five miles south of where Grandpa and Grandma lived; so when Uncle Edd would go to town for work, Aunt Lela would ride up to grandmas and stay the day. They had a wagon and team for their transportation. Uncle Edd worked in town on 12th street at the sale barn. It was often late when he would get off, but this one afternoon he was able to leave pretty early.

You could always plan on him being drunk by the time he got home. That day he picked up Aunt Lela and headed to their house. They had to cross a train track, and wouldn't you know here comes a train and it whistled and scared the horses as well as Aunt Lela. Uncle Edd whipped the old horses and Aunt Lela jumped off the wagon. By this time the train whizzed past the road, but Uncle Edd was on one side of the track and Aunt Lena on the other side. He was not sure but what the train--had not hit her; and she was not sure of how Uncle Edd was. In the break between the box cars, d they saw each other. They could not believe what had just happened.

The next morning they came to our place to tell us what had happened. Of course, we laughed and they agreed "It is funny now but it sure was not funny yesterday evening. We were frightened nearly to death!

CHAPTER 12
CHICKEN FEATHERS

Mother and daddy would work in the field so Wanda and I stayed with Grandma Keeling at the house. Grandma was tired and did not feel that good, so she laid down to rest and dropped off to sleep. I told Wanda, "Lets dress a chicken and have lunch ready when Mother and Daddy get to the house for lunch. She said that she couldn't ring that chicken's neck, and I said I would do it. So we got one all right. Catchin' chickens can be tricky.

Well, I twisted its neck and when it was dead, we began to pick the feathers. Man, it was hard. We had forgotten to put it in scalding water to make it easier to pluck, so those ol' feathers were stubborn. We had been working for a long time when Mother showed up. The first thing she noticed was that we had taken one of the layin' hens by mistake. We were feelin' bad about that. But Mother stepped in, boiled some water, and finished the pluckin'.

. . .

WHEN DADDY CAME in for lunch, she was telling him just what we had done; and he said, "Oh Mother, they was just trying to help. Don't get mad at them." Daddy was always understanding.

CHAPTER 13
WHO NEEDS A PONY?

We only had one wagon and one tricycle, and I always had to ride the wagon. I was sick and tired of having to push that thing. So, one day I told Wanda I was tired of that ol' wagon, and I intended to fix this situation.

Wanda asked what I was goin' to do, and I told her I was goin' to harness the calf up to the wagon. So, we go to the barn and I go and get all the horse gear. Then I catch the calf and I put all bridle rains and the whole nine yards on the calf. Well, the poor little thing was scared to death, But it was a very tame calf, nothing but a big pet. I was talkin' to him all the time I was latchin' her to the wagon. I jumped in and I gave the calf a swat with the rains and around the cow lot we went. And we went fast.

There was a large open well on the south side of the lot. and I went around one more time. I thought we would turn over, or go flying through the air and land in the well, and drown. So, when I got on the north side of the lot, I left that thing, jumped clear out of it. And you know what happened? The wagon turned upside down and oh what a sound it made.

Mother had gone to the other well to get our drinking water and she heard the racket, but didn't know what it was. She had two buckets of water. She set them down and came a' runnin' to see what was goin' on. When she got close enough to see us, she got a switch, got me by the arm, turned me around and let me have it.

I was laughing; and she got Wanda, turned her around, and started on her. So now Wanda begin to laugh. Mother never did make us cry,, and that upset her. So, she threw the switch down and warned u to never do that again.

I finally got the calf calmed down and took the horse's rig up off the little thing. I put them all back in the barn just where they were supposed to be. When Daddy came home we was laugh just tellin' him what a fun time we had, even if we did get a good "warm up" one more time. Daddy laughed and said, "Girls, what you two won't do has not been thought of."

CHAPTER 14

TRADING UP – GETTIN' SOME CLASS

We had an orchard. The fruit trees were so pretty when in bloom and oh how sweet they all smelled! We had apples, apricots, peaches, pears; and on the east side there was a fence full of grapes. I loved to work the orchard. I guess I got that after my daddy.

We had a team of horses, Old Cola, and Maud. They sure worked together good. We had to disk the complete area and then go over it with the **hire** [What is a "hire?"]. Daddy showed me just how close to get to the trees. He would do the close work.

Cola was real old, and when she died, Daddy bought an old mule named Jack that was the nearest to nothing I ever tried to work with. Poor Maud would try to pull the complete thing by herself. I had told daddy how lazy Jack was. but one evening I was still in the orchard, so Daddy stood there and watched old Jack for himself. So, he said he would have to do something because this is just not workin'.

Daddy gave Jack a dose of something for energy one evening, and it got real cloudy and begin to thunder. Daddy said He had better go get Jack in, because he can't get wet or he will get stiff and die. So, while daddy takes off to the field to get him, I'm thinkin' maybe that if ol' Jack would go ahead and die, it would be ok with me.

Well, it begins to rain; and by the time daddy found Jack, he was done and down. He came back to the house to tell the news.

About a week went by and Daddy was talking to a man that had a little crawling tractor. Daddy went to look at it, bought it, and the man delivered it to the house. Man, were we movin' up in the world, getting into some class now, and I could just see me setting on the seat of that thing. But Daddy gave me strict orders not to get on it until he was there to show me how to run it, and I told Daddy I'd wait for him.

Well, Saturday was my day for a test for drivin'. That was so exciting. I got the job done, and daddy said I did great. I worked the thing for two or three weeks; and one day it didn't want to start; so, when daddy came home, I told him how it was doin'. When we went to see about it,. Daddy found out real quick what it was. so, he showed me how to short across from the solenoid to the starter. and I thought that was just super.

The next day I was ready to work, but I was so short that I could not reach over the thing like Daddy did, so I went to the house and had Wanda go with me. I got inside the tractor by the cleat tracts and shorted across like daddy did. Sure enough. it worked. Only one problem. Wanda let out on the clutch, and the thing was in gear. She sure like to have run over me. Let me tell you I was moving fast and furious. So, when daddy came home, I got to tell him all about it, and he told me not to get back on that thing until he could get it fixed.

After a few years when we had quite the orchard, Daddy was going to sell the tractor; but years later, he still had it. So, after I got married, my husband George bought the tractor for me. I still have it after all these years It won't run, but some day I hope to get it fixed.

CHAPTER 15

WHO KNEW THERE WAS A SHARP SHOOTER IN ME!

Years ago, sling shots was a very poplar thing. So, when we told Daddy we wanted one, he fixed us one with a fork from a branch and a piece of inter tube. Mother and Daddy was in the field and Wanda and I was at the house with grandma one more time. I told Wanda, See that old chicken? I bet I can hit it in the head." Wanda didn't think so, Well, I got me a rock, put in that sling shot, pulled it back and I hit that old hen right in the head. She fell over and begin to kick. We kept watchin' and pretty soon she got up, slung her head, and walked off. Wanda and I agreed that was a close one.

The day went by, and when Mother went to get the eggs in, here is that old hen on the nest dead as a door nail. When Mother came in from the hen house, she asked if we what happened to the hen . Well of course I told her and said I was sorry. All she said was that if I had told her sooner we could at least have had had chicken and dumplings. I said, "Well, I didn't know that she was going to go get on the nest and die." I was just sure I was in big trouble again, but that one slipped by, thank goodness.

CHAPTER 16

TRAINING TO BE A TRADER

Daddy was a trader. One day a man came to the shop where he worked and ask if he knew anyone that had a pickup for sale or would like to do some trading, and Daddy told him, "Yes I do. So, he told the guy that after he goes home and had supper, he would bring it over to his house and let him listen to it. and the man said that is a good deal.

After supper Daddy told mother where he was going, and I asked to go and jumped in with him. The man came outside, and they talked Daddy looked at what he had to trade. I spoke up and said that our old pick up sure was making a bad sound. Daddy dropped the pan and put a meat skin between the insert and main and it sounded good. Daddy didn't say a word.

The man said, 'Well Lee, I think I will trade with you." Daddy said OK, so they signed the titles, happy with their trade.

When we got headed back home Daddy told me that if I ever go with him again, I better never volunteer anything I knew again, or I would never go with him again. I made a promise that would never happen again.

CHAPTER 17

NOT ALL LESSONS ARE LEARNED IN SCHOOL

We were going to a little two-room school where everybody knew each other. But there were two students that I remember the most: Wayne Tiner and Sammy Thomas. Both oof them liked me. Sammy went to school with me for several years. Wayne, on the other hand, was what might be called a school day sweetheart. He was really stuck on me. He used to draw my pictures and write me notes. But I wasn't interested and didn't have a lot to say to either one of them.

And then there was Larry Jackson. Because I was left-handed, Larry – like all the guys – called me "Lefty," and that made me so mad. Mrs. Enloe told them not to call me that or they would be in trouble. But on evening when I was walking home, I heard Larry running after me calling "Lefty, Lefty." I reached down, picked up a rock and threw it at him as hard as I could, and Larry ran right into that rock. It his him in the temple, and he fell like a ton of bricks. I really thought I had killed him for a minute.

When he finally got up, his first words were, "Don't tell Mrs. Enloe what happened," and he promised never to call me "Lefty" again. And he never did.

Eight years later, he came back to our area, and he was still laughing about the whole thing.

CHAPTER 18

SHORT CUTS ARE NOT FOR EVERYBODY

One night we was going to go see Uncle Edd and Aunt Lela, who had just moved down the road south of us. Wanda and I asked Daddy to let us show him our short cut down the little hill. Well, Daddy said O.K.

Wanda went first, then I went, and Daddy followed us. We hollered "Duck, Daddy, duck!" But he didn't duck quick enough. He hit that barbed-wire fence right across his forehead. Daddy said, "You fraslin' kids; you could kill a guy." We felt so bad!

When we got to Aunt Lela's and Uncle Edd's place, they doctored his head. He told them what had happened, and he never went that way again.

CHAPTER 19

A TRIP ACROSS THE TRACKS

One beautiful Saturday morning when the birds were singing, we went into town with Daddy, so we went by Aunt Sally's to ask her to go with us and of course she said she would.

On the way, we had to cross a railroad track we got to the track, we were walkin; slow and talkin'. There was a train down the track, but he was not moving. Just as we started across the track, the conductor blowed the whistle, and Aunt Sally's feet was moving so fast that she slipped on the gravel between the tracks and fell.

Rosco Crump who was setting out by the station came a runnin' and asked Aunt Sally if she was O.K. She said she was fine, but this embarrassed her.

Well and. Then here comes the conductor. "Ma'am, I am so sorry I didn't mean to scare you." Aunt Sally looked at him and smiled. "I'm O.K. You was just having fun."

Her knees were bleeding, and she hit her arm on something. We walked on up to the main part of town. Wanda and I would! augh about Rosco wanting to know if she was hurt. We teased her all that day about Rosco. He had lived in the community all his life. We all knew him and we couldn't remember his ever movin' that fast. that made it funnier than ever.

CHAPTER 20

REALLY GETTIN' "UP TOWN"

We went to school at Union Hill, a two-teacher school with first grade through the eight. There were lots of good kids, and we had lots of fun. We were all poor, but happy.

There was no school bus, so we walked to school of a mornin' and back home in the evenin'. Sometimes if Argo Dotson was grading the road, he would let us ride the grader home, and we thought that was the greatest thing there was.

But later Daddy got both Wanda and me bicycles. Boy, we felt like we was sure getting to be "up town." That didn't make us think we was better than the other kids, but we was sure the same.

We would go to eastern Oklahoma after a Christmas tree each year; so, when we told the other kids that we was going, there was four girls who wanted to go with us. We ask Daddy if they could go, and he said "Sure."

CHAPTER 21

THE TRIP FOR A TREE

We had a little A-Model pickup with a bed that wasn't big enough for nothing. Mary Nail Benion, Dana Mae Cochran, and Willa and Mary Duckworth came home with us, so we could get headed out early the next morning. The weather was pretty considering it was December, so we all loaded in the back of the pickup and off we went, all exciting and havin' fun.

Come lunch time, we stopped and ate the picnic lunch we had packed, then loaded ourselves back in the pickup. There was really no room for a tree, but we got a small one and headed back home When we got home everyone was tired and sleepy That was a fund day, one we all remember.

I was the tom boy, and I really liked to help on the farm. We had cows, calves, hogs, chickens, and horses. Of an evening I would get in the kindling chips, carry in the water, and get the lamps filled.

And every night I would get the milk pails , and away I would go to get the cows in their milkin' lots. Then it was time to let my calf in to nurse. By the time I got my first one milked, Daddy had got there.

CHAPTER 22
UP CLOSE WITH A CALF'S TOOTH

He had told me to make the calf stay on the side where I was. "But just know that it will hurt your hand." Well, I could not break the thing from running to the other side. Here I am milkin' and the calf goes to the other side. Sure enough, it spooked the old cow. Well, my hand was in the wrong place, and the calf's tooth went all the way throw my finger. The blood was pouring. I hollered at Daddy :come here quick." He left his cow and by the time he got to me, I was half way down, He caught me. He began to holler for Mother to bring some water and a wash rag. She was just across the little draw, not far. By the time she got there, he had me out of the cow lot and setting on the wagon tongue. My finger was killing me. We got the bleeding stopped, wrapped it up good, and went to finish our job well, but by that time the calves had gotten all the milk. And I sure had a sore finger for a week are longer.

CHAPTER 23
STORMY WEATHER

In the summer, the storms would start. I hated that time of the year. We did not have a cellar; so if it looked bad, we had to go over to Uncle Albert and Aunt Fannie. The roads were so bad we could not drive the car, so we would cut across the field. Sometimes we would stay in the cellar for an hour. They didn't have storm forecast like we do now; and it never did do nothing but rain. I hated for the mud to squish in between my toes.

Every night if it began to lightning Daddy would get up take the car to the top of the hill. Because the road was so bad you could not make it up the hill. He was always the first one out so he had to split the routes out to the highway.

Daddy was a trader. A man came by the place where he worked, and he had a four-wheel drive jeep. Daddy traded his little pickup for that thing, and he never had to worry about getting out no more.

CHAPTER 24

THE PIG PEN CAPER

S o, when it came time to work, we all went up to the hog pen, and when I would pour the slop in the pan. All the hogs would run over, put their heads under the slop where I was pouring, The stuff would get all over me, and that would make me so mad.

Every one of the kids standing there watching me, Aunt Shirley just stood there bawling. I looked at the others and said, "Let's set her in the pen with the old sow, and all the little ones." That old bore looked mean; he was so big. But we picked her up and set her in the pen anyway. She got louder yet. I told her that if she didn't stop that bawling. we would go to the house and leave her in there. So, in just a little while she stopped bawlin'. We told her that if she started that again, we would bring her right back up here and put her back in the pen with the hogs again. Well, they stayed at our house like a week longer and she was a god kid from that point on. About 12 years ago, she was back, and I ask her if she remembered what we did. She said, "Who could ever forget that; I remember it as if it was yesterday." We all laughed about it.

CHAPTER 25

THE BREAK IN

We went to the pie supper up at the school one night. When we got home, all the doors were locked, and we could not get in. Daddy told Mother to run over to Alberts and tell the boys to get over here. He stayed and watched.

He made me and Wanda hide behind an old washing machine that was in the yard. We was scared, and the dark didn't help nothing. We could not see a thing.

When mother got back Uncle Albert James and our cousin Hurbert had come prepared with a gun. a large machete knife and a big club. They each one got on the side of the house to watch and make sure that any intruders did not get away from them. Well, Daddy was going to kick the door in, but somebody had been in there and left the west door open when they left.

The men went all through the house but could not find a thing out of place, so they could not figure out what in the world was going on. About two weeks later Mr. Fikes told Daddy that one of his buddies and him had been in there. When Daddy ask why, he said he had heard that there was money under the floor on the south side of the house. Daddy told him that it had better never happen again, and Mr. Fikes promised Daddy that it would be the last time for him, because he was sure scared.

CHAPTER 26

DADDY AND THE DIRT DOBBER

Daddy always went to bed before Mother, and she was always hearing something outside. She ran in one night and woke daddy up and said, "Lee, get up. I heard someone outside." And he said, "Oh Mother, you always hear something." But he got up just in case.

Daddy kept his shot gun over the door, and it was always loaded. He got the gun, ran to the south door, and just about head high he fired a shot.

What Daddy didn't know was that a dirt dobber had built a nest in the barrel of the gun. When he fired it, it like to have blowed his thumb off.

So, mother had to doctor his thumb. It was not funny, but we could not keep from laughing at the way Daddy looked while getting his thumb all wrapped up.

CHAPTER 27

ME AND "THE WILD THING"

Uncle Albert had a cow that had her first calf. She was so wild, they could not milk her, so they hollered across the field for someone to come an help them. Mother hollered back and said OK.

By the time I got over there, they had the old cow in the chute and the kickers on her, but they still could not do a thing with her. I patted and talked to her. She would try to kick, but even with the hobbles on her, I could move fast enough to stay out of her way. It helped that the place was small, and I was young. Finally, I got her milked, and every evenin' I had to go over to milk that cow. And after about a week, she was trained to stand still. She sure made them a good cow, but boy, she was a wild thing.

When winter came, it was time to kill hogs. What a job that was. We had to get a fifty-five-gallon drum full of really hot water to scald the hogs in. Daddy would shut them and then cut their throats and let them bleed. Then we was ready to put them in the scalding water. So, we could get them scraped and cleaned, ready for us to start cuttin' our pieces of meat.

Daddy would leave the hams complete, then we put what we wanted to make sausage out of in a large container. We would later grind it all up and season it like we wanted it for our sausage.

Daddy would cut the bacon, and we would get the head and ears cleaned for the sauce meat. But we would not make the sauce meat, if the wind was out of the south, because they always said it would make you sick.

When we got it all cut up and covered with the sugar cane Daddy always fixed to cure the ham. We hung the hams in the smoke house Daddy would start a fire and make sure there was enough smoke going into the smoke house to keep the meat well smoked. It only took a couple days to do the trick.

We always had enough meat through the winter. In addition to the ham, we hunted rabbits and had chickens to kill and dress for a Sunday dinner. Sometimes we had a steer calf to butcher. Daddy made sure that we was going to have enough for the winter. He was a good provider.

We had our own milk cows for milk, cream and butter, and we had our chickens for eggs. We didn't have to buy those thighs, and when we had more than we needed, we sold the rest.

I loved to churn the cream to make the butter. We had molds to form the butter. We would wrap it in wax paper, and it was ready for the pantry or the market. Mother would put the clabbered milk in sacks, hung them on the cloths line and collect the whey that would drip out of it. We would whip the whey to make our cottage cheese. And it was so good.

We always had preserves and jelly to have with our hot biscuits, eggs, and bacon of a morning along with a good cup of hot coffee. The preserves was from the fruit off of our trees. Mother would make jelly and preserves that would melt in your mouth. That was those good old days.

CHAPTER 28
BALL GAMES AND MORE

When our Union Hill ball team had a home game, we could all went to see them play; but if it was an away game, we had no bus so we couldn't go. Mrs. Enloe had to make two trips with the ball players. And the boys and girls both had a game, the others had to wait back at school and find something to do.

So, one day Mrs. Enloe took the boys for their game and left the girls to wait till she got back. She told us that we could find something to do, but we were to "be nice and don't bother anything. Of course, we said we would be nice; But when she left with the boys, we found an old purse, some string, tied the string to the purse, and took off to the highway.. We put the purse on the highway and then hid under the bridge. When a car would come by, they would stop and reach for the purse, and we would pull it to us. We had more fun doing that than if we would have had going to the ball game. When Mrs. Enloe got back and found out what we had been doin', I thought we was goin' to get a spankin', but all she told us was that we better never do that again.

CHAPTER 29

MY MEMORABLE ACTING CAREER

We always had Christmas plays. One year the play was about a family, and the stage was fixed up looked just like a live-in house. It was so pretty. . Horace Golden was the dad; Dana May Cochran was the mom, and I was their little girl. Horace played and sung Christmas songs, and I set on his lap.

This was a very good play, and I will never forget it for the rest of my life. It was so real. Everybody liked it and said how good it was. and how good we all did on our parts. After the play, we had friends over for supper and games: Mary Duckworth, Wanda Keeling, Cletes and Joyce Bottoms, and Mary Nail Binion.

CHAPTER 30
DELIVERING THE MAIL

We had to go to highway 19 to get our mail. The roads were so bad no one could get up and down them in rainy weather, so they just had everyone on our road pick up their mail at the highway. Wanda and I would walk down to get our mail; and as we would go by Mr. and Mrs. Teel's house, they would say "Girls, would you mind to carry ours back to us if we have anything?" And of course, we would always tell them we were happy to. We knew when we got back to their house, Mrs. Teel would have cake, her special tea, or Kool-Aid for us we would give them their mail or tell them they didn't have any. And Mrs. Teel would say," Come in girls Rest and have a snack." We would set and talk, have our snack, and then we would tell them we better get on home or Daddy, or Mother will think something has happened to us.

When we would get home, we would laugh and say, "Well Mrs. Teel gave us a snack again." And mother had already figured that out, and how nice it was for us to get their mail for them and visit with them.

CHAPTER 31
CLIMBIN' THE SOCIAL LADDER

In 1944 daddy bought a house and had it moved. We was climbin' up the social ladder with our two bedrooms. Kitchen, living room and a big screened-in back porch.

It was forever before we got electric. When anybody would put in their order, it would take a long time to even get headed your way.

Daddy had a battery-operated stand-up radio. and he always listened to Lum and Abner and Minnie Pearl. There was another one or two he listen to. This was his pass time after supper. He got plenty of laughs from them.

In the winter when he would get home after all chores was done havin' supper, it was his time for his radio programs then his music. Daddy could play the fiddle, guitar, banjo, and the harmonica; and it was left up for me and Wanda to sing along with him. As a kid I wondered why he wanted to do that every night. But later in years I found out why.

After all these years they voted a man in as county commissioner. His name was George Collins. Everyone was very proud of that man as he was the one that got us out of the mud. Because of him, we had some pretty good road and it was so much better.

CHAPTER 32

A ROAD TRIP TO REMEMBER

When the next summer came, daddy announced we are going on vacation. We was excited! We had an old 1936 Ford. Daddy checked it all out, filled it up with gas, and we were leaving out early the next morning. We had everything packed and ready to hit the road. We got up, had breakfast, and started out, headed for Houston, Texas.

Things was going good. We got just west of Coalgate and the car sputtered and died. We was out of gas. So, daddy walk into Coalgate and got some gas. When he got back to the car, he poured it in the tank, and it started right up.

There was no more trouble at all. We was on the road like two and half days before we got to Houston.

We pulled in late that afternoon to Aunt Hattie and Uncle Felix's place. They was all waiting for us to arrive and were all very happy to see us. T they had our days planned on what we was going to do each day. So, we had supper, took our baths, and us kids played while the older ones sat and talked about old times.

After breakfast the next morning, we headed out in Aunt Hattie's and Uncle Felix's boy's pickup. It had a camper on it, so we was all fixed for the day.

He took us to the ocean. Grown men riding on the biggest turtles I had ever seen. There was like twelve of them. It was neat. When they would take off walkin', it was like a slow-motion thing and fun to watch.

We played in the sand and in the edge of the water. It was very pretty. When we were lookin' straight all we could see was the water with large waves. The sea gulls would dip down to us thinkin' we was goin' to feed them.

We took our lunch, so we got the folding tables out of the camper and got the lunch all spread. The kids were not that hungry 'because we had rather play. We took time out to eat, and then went right back to the sand and water. We found lots of seashells that had been washed ashore.

In the late evening one of our cousin Fred's little boys went and got into the camper. There was a small can of gas, and he opened it someway and drunk some of it. Well, we all gathered him up and headed to town. When we got to the hospital; the child was almost black. I thought he was going to die. They took him in and for quite some time we sat there not knowing what was going on. Finally, the doctor came out and told us he was doing good. They had pumped his stomach out. We were told we could leave in another hour are so. They wanted to watch him and make sure everything was OK. All the prayers that was being prayed saved the child's life. I know that God touched him and spared him.

When we did get to go, we headed for their house, so we could have supper and take baths. Tt had been a long day and a fun day, but a scary one too.

They had plans for the next morning. We rose early, had breakfast, and headed out again, hoping nothing exciting happened today. They took us and showed us the town. We went shopping and saw lots of large building and some beautiful homes on the way.

We stopped and got winnies and hot dog buns, chips, pop and all the extras to make hot dogs. We went to the park and had a good old hot dog cook out. We had lots of fun while they got the fire started.

After lunch, we went to see the animals. There was not that many, but we fed the big birds and the monkeys.

It was getting late, so we headed back to the house The ladies fixed supper, and we all ate then took baths. The rest of the evening, the kids all played games, while the older ones set and talked and rested.

When the morning sun came up, we was all up ready for breakfast. There was a good hot bowl of oatmeal, home-made biscuits, bacon, and sausage, with coffee and orange juice.

And just like that, it was time for us to leave. We told them goodbye and how much we enjoyed being there. We hugged all the kids and Aunt Hattie, Uncle Felix, Cousin Fred, and his wife Sherry and headed back for the place we loved, our little house in Oklahoma.

We had a good trip back home, and we was on the road for two days. When we would get tired, Daddy would stop, we would rest, and then start on the road again.

When we got home, there was lots to do. We was behind with our mowin' but Uncle Groover had taken care of the stock which was a blessing for us. Aunt Sally had taken care of the garden, which was good also, and they had extra food for the family.

CHAPTER 33
BACK TO NORMAL

Well summer was goin' very fast. it would not be long until school would be starting.

Mother had lots of sewing to do for us to have new dresses for school. So, she put aside other things to get our clothes all made. But she had to do some canning also. Wanda and I had to wash all the jars and watch the canner so it would not go too high or the pressure valve would pop off. That always scarred me because Mother had said it could blow the top off the canner. So, we watched it very close.

CHAPTER 34

THE CIRCUS AFTER THE CIRCUS

There was a circus coming to town, so Wanda and I ask Aunt Elva, Mother 'sister, and our cousin A.R. if they would like to go with us to the circus, and they said that would be fun. So, they came over to the house, and we all loaded in our car and away we went.

We could all see the black cloud that had come up, and it sure looked bad. Daddy said it would probably just be a good rain. We had to park a long way down the road, but we went on into the circus. It was not long until it sure began to rain hard. And Daddy was right, it was only a rainstorm. It was still raining hen the show was over. Mother had worn a black crape dress; and as we was walking to the car, her dress began to shrink. She would pull it down, but it kept poppin'; back up like a window shade. We laughed until we hurt. But she didn't think it was funny.

Mother will be ninety-three in August, and if you can ask her if she wants a black crepe dress, she will say, "No. I am afraid I will get it wet and shrink up. "The other night there was a circus in town and it sure enough it was raining hard. I called and asked her if she thought we should. I told her I would go get her a black crepe dress, and the only thing she said was "No I don't think so. I never want to be in that kind of mess again. And we both had a big laugh.

CHAPTER 35

A PROUD DAY, A SAD DAY, AND LOTS OF MEMORIES

Well, when it was time to graduate from the eighth grade. It was a sad time, because that was the last year for some of us to be together. Our school colors were yellow and black, and our motto was **NOT THE END BUT THE BEGINING.** We each had a reading to give, but there was only a few: Corene Campbell, Cleta Bottoms, Dana Mae Cochran, Wanda Keeling, and myself. I think that was all.

We was leaving lots of good memories behind, and we were leaving a place that had been a part of our lives for all those years. There was our outside pump with the long pipe that the water flowed through. The pipe had holes where the water came out and we got our drink. There was two out buildings: the girls on the north side, and the boys was on the south. We had a basketball court just south-west of the school house, and a softball field due south of the school house. We also had a merry-go-round that we all loved. I had made lots of tracks around that whole place since the first grade. And I saw lots of kids come and go; but we stayed put and I am sure proud, because Daddy always said a rolling stone never gathers no moss.

All the way through school we would have the County Superintendent. His name was Mr. Michell, and he visited all the schools every month. Mr. Mitchell, he had a bad leg and used a cane. One day when he came out, he asked us to spell *Pontotoc,* and not one of us could spell it; so, he wrote it on the blackboard and told us when I come out next month, we all had better know how to spell Pontotoc. We begins to learn how to spell it, and it was not that hard Mrs. Enloe made sure everyone in the room knew how to spell it and helped us know that it was a name of a town in Mississippi close to a place called Tupelo.

The world globe hung from the ceiling, and it could be lowered with a heavy cord. We pulled it back up to the ceiling where no one could get at it. Only the teacher was allowed to lower it.

When the erasers to be dusted, only two students at a time was allowed to dust the. We took them to the east side of the schoolhouse and pounded them on the wall of the school house.

When we would go to carry in the wood, only one row could go at a time. But we all had our turn. It was lots of fun; and in the warm weather, we went real slow to kill time and stay out of the classroom, but when it was really cold, we got out and back a lot quicker.

One of the best times was when it was time for the fair. There were a lot of us in 4-H and we had a ball. There were dress shows, and demonstrations about how to make cookies or cakes from start to finish.

But one thing we did not enjoy at the end of that school year was knowing that when we went to another school it was goin' to be a completely different way of life.

CHAPTER 36
LOTS OF CHANGE IN LATTA DISTRICT HIGH SCHOOL

Sure enough, when we got to Latta District we had a lotta changes. There were like 30 kids in one class. But we all had to learn how to handle it.

But the teachers were all there to help, just like the little two room school. And the kids were all very friendly and good to everyone. We got to know all the kids in the high school, not just the 9th grade, which made it feel like one big family. The bus did not come down our road, so we had to ride out with Daddy of a morning and go over to Aunt Bessie's and Uncle Traves' place. Our cousin Roy Wayne went to Latta, so we all rode the same bus which worked out good.

Before school was out Aunt Bessie and Uncle Traver moved, and there went our bus stop. But we had made friends with Betty Landers so we would ride to her house of a morning with Daddy, and that was our bus stop for the rest of that year.

Then the next year, the bus came right up to our house which made it much better for Daddy and us too. There was a little red-headed girl in the first grade, and she took a likin' to me. She had to set by me on the bus of a morning and of the evening. her name was Janetta Lane, and I will never forget that little girl. After about two years her family moved and went up north somewhere. Several years later when she came back to visit, she and her mother hunted me up. Her hair was still red and still had her freckles. But she had lost her dad.

The 10th grade of school was very exciting. I was playin' basketball, but I was not a real good player. For one thing I was shy and didn't like to wear the shorts.

In our class we had one are two that thought they was better than the others, at least that was the way I felt about them. One was Billie LaFollette. Her dad was a preacher. She was a very pretty girl; and as I got to knowin' her better, she was not really stuck-up; that was just her ways.

There was a store across the road. and we could go over there at lunch time. It was owned by Mr. and Mrs. Roper, and they also had children going to school there. In fact, from time to time I see Betty their daughter who still lives here in Ada. There was several of us kids that was freshman when I started there that all went through the four years of High school together. At the end of the four years, you knew them pretty we.

One girl Haskelene Griffin called me Stinky, and I called her Buzzard. That was all we ever called one another. She was always a very jolly girl, full of life. Mrs. Bunch, the English teacher, was on her all the time, and so was the Math teacher Mr. Cleghorn. Buzzard he was forever doing something to get into trouble. She would call the math teacher the "old bachelor," which he was because he had never married. But he was really fun to be around.

We had typing in the basement. Marchine Eaton our teacher a very sweet lady, always easy to get along with. There was no class this one morning, and we decided to hide in the closet down there during study hall. Well guess what, we were lucky, nobody missed us. It was a wonder some of the other kids didn't ask where we was, but no one said a word.

CHAPTER 37

KEEPIN' BUSY IN THE SUMMER

In the summer that year Wanda my sister wanted to learn to crocket. There was a lady that lived close to Grandma Keeling there in town. And daddy said if she would teach us kids, we could pay her with eggs, milk, and butter. That sounded good to the little lady, so we got thread and needles.

Well Wanda learned to crochet, but I was left-handed, and she could not teach me. But later years Wanda got a mirror, and we set in front of it and watch how to do left-handed was real exciting for me. I love to do it even until this day. When I am depressed, I get my needle and thread and get busy. I have also learned to knit.

CHAPTER 38
WHISLIN' NEIGHBORS AND THE FORTUNE TELLER

Aunt Todd, Daddy's sister, was an old maid, and across the street from her and Grandma was an old bachelor named Tom. He would get in the yard and just whistle up a storm. And when Todd would be in her yard, she would whistle up a storm. Wanda and I told her he was whistlin' to her and she was whistling to him. We teased Todd all the time about him. She would just laugh.

In the next block up from Grandma lived a red headed woman. They said she read fortunes with cards. So, one day Wanda and I decided that we would go and let her tell us our fortunes. Wanda went in first and all the time she was in there I was wondering what kind of a lie she was telling her.

So, when it was my time, I got up a little slow not knowing rather I really wanted to go in there are not. But I went in, and she begin. First thing she said you really don't care for boys, do you? And I said, "No ma'am, not really." She looked at me and said that one day there the right one would come along. And it looks like it might be a year maybe a year and a half. But the boy you will fall in love will be tall, thin, blond headed and a real smart guy.

So, when we started back to Grandma's house, I was telling Wanda what she told me, and I said that I couldn't hardly believe that. Then Wanda began to tell me that she had told her there was going to be a death in the family like six months or maybe a little longer. And sure enough, Grandma passed away. So that made me think maybe she could be right about me too. But there sure would have to be lots of changing in my mind.

CHAPTER 39

THE 10TH GRADE: MY FORTUNE TURNED

And sure enough, about a year later when I was in the 10th grade, it happened. Wanda's old boyfriend Sonny Pierce told his friend George that he knew where there were two good-looking girls. Sonny told him, "If we go out there and make a date with them, I want to go with the blond one," and George said that was o.k. with him. So, one evening here they come. We talked for a while, and we made a date to go to the movie.

Well, I was not pleased with my date at all. When they started to leave, they said they were coming on Saturday at 6:30 to take us to another movie.

When they left, I told Wanda I won't go with Sonny if he's the last boy on earth. Sonny was Wanda's old boyfriend anyway, so Wanda said, "Ok, I'll tell you what we will do. About the time for them to be here, I will go over to the wash house to feed the kittens. You tell Sonny where I am and have him come over to scare me. Then you and George go up the road, and tell George that you are not going with Sonny, that you are going with him."

And that is what I did. -When George and I got back, Sonny told me to get in the back seat with him, and my answer to him was "No! I am going with George tonight." It made Sonny mad, but sure made me feel good. It all worked out perfectly.

And guess what, that was thin and blond-headed, and he was a very clean-cut boy.. So, what the fortune teller told me really come true.

CHAPTER 40

GEORGE WAS "IN", SONNY WAS "OUT"

About three weeks went by, and George came out to the house, and we played dominoes. It was like 7:30 when he left. The next day Sonny called the school and ask for me. When I went to the phone, he said, "I thought you might like to know that George was out with another girl last night, and it was late when he got back. And I just said, "Oh, sure enough? And his answer was yes.

I didn't tell him that George was at my house. But when George came out that night, I told him Sonny had called me at school to tell me he was out late last night. George said, Well I will fix that."

Now, George and Sonny shared an apartment; so when Sonny got home. George told him that he needed to find him somewhere else to stay. George told him that he was at my house and he knew that Sonny was only tryin' to make trouble. So, Sonny had to pack his little bit of stuff and find some where to rest his head.

He didn't even have a job, so it was hard on him, because he had nowhere to go.

CHAPTER 41

THE CARNIVAL, THE TRUCK, AND GEORGE'S LUCK

There was a carnival in town, and George and I went. We rode the rides, played the games, and when we started home we discovered he had lost the keys The old truck was like a forty eight with the lock on the wheel. So, we walked over to his sister Estalene's house on third street. When we got there his dad was there. We were asked to come on in. When we stepped in, George introduced me to his family. His dad spoke up and accused George of robbin' the cradle. That made me so mad. Well then after a while his dad told him he could use his car to take me home.

As we started to leave, I told them it was nice to meet them all and in returned they said "nice to have met you." So, we left so I could get home on the right time.

When we got home, we had to tell Mother and Daddy that we had lost the keys to the truck. But I said I had met his dad and his sister and that they were all nice. I also told them what Mr. Smith ask George about robbin' the cradle, and Mother and Daddy thought that was funny, but it made me mad.

George said he had better go so he could get up early in the morning and get to the supply store and get me a switch for that old truck, before he had to go to work. Of course, I told him be careful and I will see you, and he said yet in a night or two.

We was goin' to the drive-in one night, and on Oak Street there was a black that cat run across in front of us. I begged him to turn and not go across the path, and he said that there was nothing to that. On top of that, it was Friday the thirteenth.

We went on to the movie, and if he didn't win two hundred and fifty dollars! He said, "See what good luck that was.". He gave me the money and the next day I took it to the bank and that is where it stayed the whole time he was in Service.

CHAPTER 42

GEORGE GETS INTRODUCED TO CAMP ROBERTS, CALIFORNIA

It was like two months later, and he had to leave for the Service. They sent him to Camp Roberts California. Oh, he was sure home sick. He had really took a likin' to Mother and Daddy and of course, me too. He told me he fell in love with me the first time he came out to the house. And there was love there for him from me also. He was just a super guy.

He had an accident while he was there. His feet slipped out from under him and he took the hide off of both legs from his knees down on the gravel. At the hospital, they gave him a penicillin shot. As it turned out, he was allergic to it, so they had to give him another shot to take care of the first one. That one made him break out and swell up somethin' bad. It took like three days to get things back like it should be.

He was doing fine, and about two weeks later he took pneumonia and they had to put him back in the hospital for like two weeks. Then if they didn't do the same thing again. They gave him the same shot he was allergic to. And again, they had to give him the shot that go rid of the allergy. He sure had lots of bad luck while he was there.

After like six months I guess they decided that he was too expensive for them. George's dad couldn't work, so his check had to go to his dad. Anyway, they got all the paper work done and sent him home. Everybody was happy he was back, and George was proud he had served.

CHAPTER 43
ROUGH LIFE

When George and all his brothers and sisters were still very young, s they were sent to the State Home, because his dad could not take care of them. His mother had run off with another man. Later Mr. smith married another woman, and they had three girls. After a bit she left him, with the girls.

As time went by, Mr. Smith had been saving money to get a lawyer. Finally he went to court and got George and his sisters back from the State Home. But when he got them back, the mom stepped in again. All the kids said they would go live with mom. But George told the judge he would run off before he would live with her after what she has done. So, the judge told Mr. Smith, George could live with him. I am glad, because if he hadn't stayed in the area, I probably would never have met him.

I remember the time Mom called Mr. Smith and told him her and the kids were hungry. They had no food. Well George told him and his dad went to the grocery store and got a pickup load of food and took it over to the house. When Mr. Smith walked in, this man was behind the door. George said this man knocked his dad in the head. George run to the pickup to get his dad's gun. By this time, Mr. Smith was up and he went through the house but the man had gone out the back door.

Well, they went to file charges on the man. And Mr. Smith knew who he was and they told what had happened and they said we don't have enough proud of what happened so we can't do anything about it.

CHAPTER 44

A HARD LIFE, BUT A SOFT HEART

George had a hard life, but he didn't let that stop him from becoming a good person. He liked to give if he never did get a thing. He was always happy. He tried to make every day happy.

George got a job working for Don Owens Trucking Company. He would drive the trucks and also do the machine work on them. He was a man that could do anything and was not afraid of hard work. He worked there for quite a long time. He was uploading pipes one day and putting' them on the pipe rack when they begin to all roll before he could get out of the way. They hit him, knocked him down and broke his leg. It was luck that was all it did to him because they were all coming right to him. He said the Good Lord was there watching over him.

When he came to the house to tell me what had happened, I could not believe it there he was in the cast and on crutches. I knew that I sure loved him then because that made my heart hurt.

Wanda and Betty had two old boys that wanted to go steady with the; but Daddy said no you are not going with them. This weekend we was going to go to town and they pulled up. and daddy told them we are leaving. So, Daddy put the car in gear and we headed down the road. Daddy said this Henry will go farther on a gallon of gas than the thing they are driving. We headed down toward Roff, got down the road about five miles daddy turned right with those boys right behind us. we went down like six or seven mile and it was dead end road. And here the boys were, still right behind us. So, we took off again when we got to the highway Daddy said we'll we will lose those boys some way somewhere. And sure enough. we ditched them somewhere or they got the message, one.

Daddy just laughed when he got the little red Henry. He went to the new car dealer and asked him what his low dollar was. And The man told him. Now Daddy wore old overalls that mother had patched and the put another patch over that patch. He looked like he didn't have a dime. He looked the car over again and he said to him is that the best you can do on this thing? And the man said," I tell you what I will do, a one-time offer, and he popped daddy a low price and Daddy said, "I will take it! Service it out for me and I will wait.

Oh, you talk about a man trying to get out of the offer. Daddy said, "No, you sold it." He pulled the money out of his pocket and paid cash for it. And the man said, "I did not think about you taking it. I priced it too cheap." Daddy said, "Well next time you will be a little bit careful. Daddy had a big laugh because the man just thought he was just looking. Daddy said this will teach him not to think a man don't have no money because his clothes are patched.

Well, a week had gone by and George was so tired of not being able to do a thing. He decided to start coming out and taking me and Wanda to school every morning and picking us up in the evening. We told Mr. Stegall what we was going to do, and he said that would be fine.

Well, the girls who lived out our way wanted to ride to school in back that was fine we didn't mind at all, so one day George thought how funny it would be to fix up a hot seat well he went to the supply store and got a switch to put a hot wire from the switch to the spring in the back seat. The next morning, we made our round to pick up Leela Roddy, Betty Landers, and Tommy Lancaster. We was headed for the school, and George hit the switch and Leela was setting on the side where it hit Ann. she just had a fit and the others said they didn't feel a thing

The girls switched seats, and George flipped a switch again. That time Betty was sitting there and she said it was something, because it bit her too. So, they switched seats again, and Tommy got hit and said that it was bad. By this time, we was at school, and George could not keep it no longer he had to tell them what he had done and we had a big laugh out of it

Mother did not drive, so George could come out and get her take or to the laundromat. He stayed there and helped her put the clothes in and wash them and then rinse them, load them back in the car, and to the house they would come. He would carry them to the clothesline, and then he would help hang every piece on the line. He was a very special person. He loved my mother and daddy. It was not Mr. and Mrs. Keeling; it was mother and dad.

CHAPTER 45

THE DAY WE ALMOST HAD SMOKED HAMS

One Sunday we all went to see aunt Minnie and Uncle Lou. So, George came out to our place before we got home. He got the milk pails and went to the cow lot to milk, so we would not be late for going to church.

Well, he smoked and thought nothing about throwing the cigar down in the lot. He was almost done when we got home. We finished helping him, then we headed to church.

When church was over, we headed for home. When we pulled up in the driveway, we saw sparks but could not figure out what in the world it was. When we got close, we found out it was the cow lot was just smelterin' the cow fodder was on fire underneath it all. We like to have never got that stuff out. We shoveled, poured water on it, and had a hard time getting the stuff put out. We teased George a long time about that, and of course he just smiled and laughed. He had a laugh like no one else.

CHAPTER 46
THE "TAIL" OF A FIRE

After school one evening we was going into town on West Main. Before we got to the first railroad tracks, George said he smelled something, and I said I did too. Well in a little while we found out what it was. He sometimes rolled his cigarettes, and they always dropped little sparks of tobacco. And that is exactly what happened. When he realized what it was, he pulled over real quick and grabbed the tail of his shirt. It was on fire.

We had another big laugh, and of course we had something else to tease him about. But he didn't mind. He said, "Oh that will be something we can tell everyone," and that is what we did.

Every weekend, we would plan where we was going, and what we was going to do. We had some new place to go each week ; lots of places to explore and take in.

We heard about the Governor Brown's Mansion at Sasakwa, so we said that would be a good place to go. We began to talk at school about goin' to the Governor Brown Mansion in Sasakwa. Well Lela, Betty, Tommy, Wanda, George and myself decided to take a sack lunch and go see what it really looked like. So, early on Saturday we all got together and headed out.

We got there; and sure enough it, was a very pretty house, but it had begun to run down. The stair case was one of a kind. It would have been a very beautiful house to redo. There was a cellar on the west side. and we decided that would be a perfect place to eat our lunch. We got the tablecloth out and put out our lunch. Everyone had something different to eat, and by the time we got it all put together we had a great meal. We eight , got back in the car, and headed for home. We always had a lot of clean fun. .

CHAPTER 47
DOIN' LIFE TOGETHER

On November the 26th, George as me to marry him, and I said "yes", because by this time I thought I knew him. and I thought he seemed to know me well enough to live together the rest of our lives. So, we set the date.

We lived in a little apartment for three weeks; when my cousins Else and Ruby called and said they had bought a place in town and if us kids wanted to move in the house and keep it up, we could have rent free. Boy, what a deal! So I said we "sure, "went to Mr. Rhyne's used furniture store on West Main, and got a living room suit, a stove, an ice box, a bedroom suit and new curtains. And I still had money left from the two hundred and fifty dollars that we won at the movie. Oh yes, the most important thing: we got a kitchen table and chair

Things was going real good. We was happy as little love birds. But then one day – it had not been two months – Ruby called and said she and Else o don't like living in town and they wanted to come back home. All we could say was, "OK, we will find something else, I guess.'

one evening George and I was standin' in the yard at Don Owen's place, and he saw a little house that was empty; so he pulled the old truck into the station, and he ask the man that was out there "could you tell me who owns the little house right over there?" The man said "I sure can tell you. It's me." George asked if he wanted to sell it and he said he did. Then George asked how much and when the man told , George said, "I will let you know tomorrow or the next day."

The next day George went to the house mover Sam Fordice and asked him how much to move the house out on Mother's and Daddy's property. So, he then went to talk with Orval Price at Witherspoon Finance and asked about getting money to buy the house and gettin' it moved. Orval said they could sure do that for us when George got home that night, we was building air castles, imaginin' what our first home would be like. That was one big step for us.

George paid the man for the house and then got Sam Fordice and said, "Let's get that thing moved." Sam said he would move it in the morning, and George told him just where we wanted it. George had to put flags out where for the front to be.

The work was beginning and things was looking good. We could not seem to wait to see what the little house was going to look like setting there on the hill.

We got it moved and we thought things was just what we needed. Then we woke up to the fact that we had no water. So again, George goes down to Orval and told him our problem and Orval said we had to get someone to drill a well. So we did.

But we had no bathroom. George's dad built us a little out house which was just what we needed. We had to use that little house for several years while we paid off all our debts. It took a lot of hard work, but we got it done.

When we moved all our things in the little house, it sure was a tight squeeze, but we got it all in there. It all Looked real pretty. We was very happy and excited about how fast things was coming together.

CHAPTER 48
STILL IN SCHOOL

I was still in school, and I had lots of fun at school, but I think I had more after I got married than before. Like one day we went to the study hall which was up on the top floor. There was a fire escape on the west side of the building, so we decided we would skip study hall and set out on the platform at the mouth of the fire escape chute.

Things was going fine until Mr. Stegall passed by the fire escape chute on the ground. He could hear us talking because our voices was carryin' down the chute. He said "I don't know who is up there, but you better come down. The other girls told me to go first, because "he won't whip you."

So, I said "OK" and I slid down the chute and landed right between his feet. He looked down and said "I would have never dreamed of that being you.' He looked at me with a grin and said, "get to that study hall and don't let it happen again. Then he told the rest of the girls to get down "right now" and about five more came down to meet him. He told them that they had better not let this happen again. And nobody got spanked.

CHAPTER 49
THE SUPPER GAME

Several of the girls from school decided we needed to cook supper. It was what you called "find out who you was goin' to marry." The girls talked about it all day at school, and everybody knew when they were goin' to do.

George said he didn't mind and poor George went down to Mother's and Daddy's hose that night. He was so sweet and good to me.

That night all the girls was to cook with hands behind you. Then they was to set two plates down, one for themselves and the other for who you was goin' to marry. They were to have it all ready to set on the table at 12:00 sharp. But guess what, they all got their plates down and supper on the table but no one came to eat with them. I laughed and told them, "Don't guess you girls are goin' to get married." And we had a big laugh.

CHAPTER 50

WASHINGTON: THE TRIP OF A LIFETIME

Our trip to Washington was the high moment of my school years. We went to the Tomb of the Unknown Soldier at Arlington Cemetery. They have a guard on duty 24/7 all the time, 365 days a year

There were so many graves of soldiers, and that day they had a burial while we were there. They carried the body in a carriage pulled by horses.

We also went to the mint place where they make money. I couldn't believe all those bills being printed. That was a real interesting place. We went to Lincoln Memorial and took several pictures.

I would not trade that trip for a fortune. But I was sure home sick. I told George when I got back that he didn't have to worry about me leaving him, never again.

CHAPTER 51
"NO BEER HERE"

We were home on the weekend, and I looked out the window and I saw Uncle Jodie and Aunt Dess headed for our house. We went to the door and saw Uncle Jodie had beer with him. I asked George awe were goin' to do? George told me you tell him we don't drink and we don't want it in the house. "Just tell him nice like and he won't get mad/. So I told them they was welcome here anytime, but not the beer. And he said, "Ok h I'll leave it in the truck." And he never did bring any more back to our house as many times as they came.

CHAPTER 52

A TRAGIC DAY

We got a call from Uncle Luther telling us that Aunt Mammie had got shot and killed by her own brothers. He told us when the funeral was and where. well we went to Linsay to pick up Uncle Joe and Aunt Dess, then came back and picked up Mr. Smith and the girls. George and I lit out to go to Crowder. We left the evening before the funera we could be down there with Uncle Luther.

When we got there, Uncle Luther said Aunt Mammie's brothers was still on the loose. They had shot and wounded the colored man that worked there, but he was able to tell them all about what happened.

Came time to go to bed, there was so many of us, we had to make pallets on the floor. But I was scared to death thinkin' the boys could come back during the night.

But then the following morning we found out both brothers had been arrested. that was a big load gone off our minds knowing they were behind bars.

We all got ready to go to the funeral home, but poor old Uncle Luther was so upset, but after the funeral things begin to look better to him and he came right out of it. He was a strong man.

CHAPTER 53
AND MORE SADNESS

We hadn't hardly got over that shock, and Mr. Smith had a heart attack and passed away about three months later on February the 13th, 1954. George and I had gone to Chickasaw to see his sister Estelene and her husband Clyde. Don and Hazel Owens, George's boss, and his wife, came over and got the girls until we got home.

We went down to see George's dad, and Mr. and Mrs. Bob Adams told us what had happened. So, we rushed over to the funeral home; but It was getting late and they told us to come back in the morning.

When we got home, we started makin' phone calls. Aunt Jewel and Uncle Tom was to leave the next morning to go home to California, but when we told them of what had happened, they stayed for the funeral.

Oh, what a sad time. The three girls were left without a father. My mother and daddy done had taken in the oldest girl Lorene. And only three weeks before, Mr. Smith had asked me that if anything happen to him, would we keep the girls and raise them like I was raised, and I told him we sure would and the other two came t live with us.

Well, we sure had our hands full: house payment, car payment, TV payment, now a funeral expense. I ask George how in the world will we make it. His answer was "Oh if we work and try, God will see us through."

CHAPTER 54
A NEW ADVENTURE BEGINS

While I was finishin' school, George was working for Don at his trucking company. I would go from school to help George at Don's shop where I cleaned parts and swept floors. And for some time, we had been bringing a bunch of stuff to George's dad to salvage out and make a little money.

I got out of school in 1953. Then in February 1954 is when we lost George's dad,

After the funeral, George went and told Don that he was going to give him a two weeks' notice, because he was going to try it on his own. Don said he understand, but told George he hated to lose him because he was a good worker. "But if you need to go ahead and start workin' on your own that is fine with me, because you have to see if you can make workin 'on not, you can always come back. You will have a job."

George said he appreciated that, "but are you sure it won't leave you in a hard spot."

Don told George that he would make it. And then he said, "I'm worried about you. This is going to be hard." George told him that he understood "but God will provide for us."

And Don said, "yes, I He will, and I hope the best of luck in the world for you two. And if you ever need me, just let me know." That was a very helpful to me.

Well, we opened the doors of George Smith Salvage about the 20th of February, 1954. We had an adventure ahead of us, for sure, a big one.

We started out with a 1-ton truck and a hand winch. What a job! But we was determined to get it done. The city would give us calls and also the Highway Patrol. They all became like family with us. I would make a banana pudding we will take it to the ADA Police Department and the Sheriff's Office; not bribing them, but showing them, we appreciate it what they done

Well, there we were with two cars, a pickup truck, no money in our pockets or the bank, and lots of bills. But we had lots of love and determination.

Mr. Smith had saved all the flour sacks. a 55-gallon barrel of them, still with the seams , so George and I took all the seams out and re-washed them. I got busy makin' the girls some new dresses. I took a Sears book, looked at the dresses and cut patterns to make them like the ones in the book.

George was v good at taken' the sack into town and match the color I needed for the clothes. It was quite a job, because I had never finished a dress before, Everything I had ever started, Mother would have to finish. But it had come time for me to do things for myself, and I did. It was an experience that I will never forget. It was a good feeling for me. I knew I had to do .it, and God was my helper or I would not have ever got it done.

George got material to match several dresses and he got the buttons to match the thread. He did a super job. God blessed us so much from day one, and it was not very many days until the girls had some new dresses and they looked very nice even if I did make them. We didn't have money to buy the patterns so I had the girls to stand up and I took a newspaper and got these scissors and cut a pattern, but I got the job done.

We was lucky Mr. Smith had a singer sewing machine which I still have.. It's a little used up, but still in the family.

CHAPTER 55
ANOTHER HOUSE TO MOVE

Well now, we had to have a bigger house. our family had gotten bigger and very quick. George found a three-room house, and we moved it next to the two-room house so we could have five rooms. God was taking care of us just like George said He would.

One day a man came to the shop and said "George, you are working on your house, aren't you? And George said we were. The man then told George that they had took some square ceiling tile down to the dump, " I'll bet there is enough to fix your house." So George came and told me he was goin' to take a good look at the ceiling tile When he came back, what a happy person he was, He had a truck load of ceiling tile, and he was goin' back after more. He got that second load and went and got another one. What a blessing that was to have plenty to fix the house and some leftover.

George was right: be good and honest, and God will see that we make it. God will always take care of us.

CHAPTER 56

JUST A LITTLE MORE?

We was renting property from Mrs. Daggs on what is called now sandy Creek Drive, back then it was the old highway 13. And how things changed. We stayed right there, and business began to grow. We got more cars and pickups. God was doing great things for us.

We got a hay truck and began to haul hay at night. I was the truck driver. George and his brothers Ray and Fred was the loaders.. George said we couldn't get enough hay on the truck, so he got busy and built an extension on the truck. I didn't think it would work, that it would just break off. But I got it hooked on their good, and that night we went over by Vanoss to get a load of hay. It worked good, until we started out of the hay field and got to a little hill, and sure enough, it broke. We had to redo our load, and after that we forgot about the extension.

CHAPTER 57

MOVIN' ON

We was loading hay, carrying it, and putting it in the barn for five cents a bale; , but we was making money. It was hard earned, but that made us strong and more determined than ever to make it

I told George I didn't mind the work; but if it is the Lord's will, next year things will be better, and we won't have to do this for a living. And sure enough, that was the last summer we had to haul hay. Our salvage business was doin' much better and things was really good for us

George and Randy our helper would work at night, and I would keep the fire going in the old wood stove for them. I would hold a large piece of cardboard up between them and the north side of the room so they could feel the heat. Every little bit I would go out to the car and make sure Judy and Jean were still covered up and that they was good and warm. They would be close together like little puppies.

CHAPTER 58
FIGHTIN' MY FEARS

Some nights I would stay at home if I had something that I just had to do. When it would start to get dark, I would get sheets and put them over the windows. I was scared and I begin to see that the girls was getting to be afraid, too. They knew this was not going to work. d so I just put the fear out of my mind and said "Lord help me too not be afraid." And it was not long until I was not afraid of the dark or nothing else. God saw how afraid I was and I had been that way during my growin' up years. But that is the Lord that we are serving. There's nothin' too big or too small for him to help if we only ask.

CHAPTER 59

ALL WORK, NO PLAY? NOT FOR US

We were blessed with lots of friends: Mitchell John, Wayne Smith, Joe Cutrale, Willie Pitts, "Jellystone: Jack Cliff, Rock Northcutt, and Tim Stone. I know I left someone out. but they were all true friends with us. Joe and his wife Susie would bring their kids to our house and we would play games. What a good did the time we would have. Woody and Pam would also come out with their kids.

We had some good memories.

Even the work gave us special memories. We was on a wrecker call one night. There was a pickup in a deep ditch. George took the line down the bank, and I was pulling cable off so it would not get over the bull gear. George dropped the line hand, and the cable on my end knocked my glasses off. I began to scream, and he's runnin' up the bank to see what was wrong. I told him to shine the light, "but don't step on my glasses." He found them about 6 feet from where I was at. He picked them up, twisted them a little, and gave them to me, He said we would get them straightened the next day, and we finished the job.

CHAPTER 60
STEPPIN' IT UP

As time went by. we got a truck and put a power winch on it. Wee was stepping it up, but we still knew who was behind us. God was with us all the way. We always had food, clothes on our back. a good place to call home

CHAPTER 61

JOB AND FAMILY TOGETHER

When we went on wrecker calls, we loaded the two girls in the old truck and take off. Then our girl was born in 1955, so we had three girls. And we had lots of fun with them. If we was working or playing, Georgie was the life of the party, whether we were home or in the truck

CHAPTER 62
FINALLY, A LITTLE BOY

Then we got our boy Willie (William). He was really a spark for us all; never a quiet moment. But we would all still take the lead in the old truck when we had a job. We had a baby bed at the shop while I worked answering the phone and making tickets. And then I had my sewing machine there to make the kids' clothes. There was no idle time, just happy times.

Well, author child came, and it was a boy. George named him Robbie. We was a good size and happy family. There sure was never a dull moment.

Robbie could not leave the electric drill alone. One day he got it going and caught his shirt tail in it. Randy ran and unplugged the drill just before it got his belly. Believe me, we never had to tell him to leave it alone again.

And undoin' plugs out of the wall was another thing he was always doin'. We spanked him, but it didn't help. So, one day he tried to unplug and plug it in again, but he got his finger too close and it bit him. We called the doctor, and he said just to watch him close for 30 minutes to an hour, that he would be fine. And we never had a problem out of him again with plugs.

An one day we heard them in the back laughing. We went to see what they was doin'. Well, Robbie was on the chain host, and Willie had him hanging all the way up to the top of the building. What they didn't think of! Just boys for you, but they made me turn gray-headed.

CHAPTER 63

AND THE FUN GOES ON – MORE GRAY HAIRS

Georgie got a new motorcycle but it had no brakes. When he was comin' toward the house, I did not think he was goin; to stop. Then Jean runs out there, mounted the thing and got her burned. It was bad for the week. Jean and Judy was just plain little girls, always easy to please. I loved those girls even if they were just George's half-sisters.

Georgia got the boys a go cart, something Willie had been wanting, It was a single seat, but Robbie wanted a double seat. So one day John Wayne Smith, one of the local trappers, was on duty out here. Robbie asked him if he wanted to go for a ride. John said sure, and they left headed east on top of a hill. Robbie makes a fast donut turn and John flew off. John got back on, came back to building and said "I didn't think about the kid makin; a quick turnaround.

But here other love was music. She said, "Daddy, I want a piano." He said he would get her one. And if you learn to play it, I will take you and let you pick out a new one. And he got her an old upright.

She began playing and about two months later, there was a music recital at Tupelo 4-H club. She entered to play "Barrell House Bessie." We went, and Mother and Daddy went with us.

She went up to play and she got first place! We was all proud of her. When we got in the car to start home, George said "Sissie, I guess me and you be going to get a piano." Well, the next week they went and she picked out a new Corona. Our kids have done nothin' but make us proud of them. They liked to spin their tires a little, but what kid didn't. But they never got a ticket. We always told them "If you do something and get in jail, don't call us. You will have to set it out You make your bed,, you sleep on it.

Well, they growed up, got married off, left home and they never moved back. They all have their own places. And we are very proud of them.

Then our grandkids started coming. And we enjoyed that very much. George gave every one of them a nickname that he would call them by. In all, we had seven grandkids.

One day George went to bid on a car, and he took all seven with him. They was not that big, and I was afraid he would have trouble with them, but he made it fine.

Then here came cancer George had it in his lungs. What a bad time that was. He would ride with the boys in the big old truck after he got so sick, he could not drive.

We lost him in 1990. After he passed, the boys would say when they went on a big rig run it seemed like Daddy was right there by them.

Willie took his big truck and little truck and started his own business. He is doing very good, I am proud of him and Connie.

Robbie and Georgie is still at the salvage and wrecker. I am now eighty five and still go to the office every day and dispatch calls after closing and on weekends. I go to church Wednesday nights and Sunday and Sunday night. I put the phone on someone else to take the calls. It has been a good life, and God has been our guide all the way.

CHAPTER 64

A COLD NIGHT IN THE CHURCH

We was still at Daggs on Sand Creek Drive that used to be Highway 13/ George went to a grocery store that was selling out, and he bought so much it was unreal. It had rained for about two days, and it was still raining. The clouds looked really bad. This was in October.

I went down and old Mother and Daddy that I was going to tell George that they was talking about closing the highway on account of high water. so they all loaded in my car and away we went.

My parents had had my sister's baby since she and her husband had gone to town to wash clothes. We went and told them that they was thinkin' about closin' the road We told them we was goin' to go to tell George.

Later, on the way home, we got to the bridge and they had closed it down. There we were, no place to go and it was as cold as could be. Daddy said he had a key to the church house, there we all headed over there. Daddy went in, got the stove on, and in a little we all went in and slept in the church that night.

CHAPTER 65
THE PREACHER'S BUS

George had worked on a preacher's bus, and they had a bunch of kids. George said when the preacher came to get his bus, we would give him a bunch of groceries.

When the preacher came to pick up his bus, George helped him loaded his stuff, and he told George I would go get the money for fixing the bus and be. Well, we waited and waited, but he never came back. We come to find out they just left town, George said "It's their loss and our gain." Whenever anybody y got to him, that's what he would say. We were not the only ones to lose on this deal. The preacher got to Ken Shipley for a new tv too.

CHAPTER 66
HITTIN' THE BOTTLE ONE TIME TOO MANY

L.L. Conley worked for us when we was moving from the business. The state bought our eight acres to put the four lanes in on the old road. He drove the truck and trailer loaded with crushed cars to Oklahoma City.

One day Randy had Conley to help with the chain on the crane. Randy took him way high in the air, and Conley was afraid of heights. He was screaming all the way up.

We had a boy working for us George asked him one day Charlie, you're not drinkin' on the job, are you? "Of course, he said no, so when he went to lunch George told Randy they were goin; to find Charlie's bottle. Well, they found it,. George opened it up, put some had brake fluid , mixed it good and put back under the machine rags just like it was. When Charlie came back from lunch, we didn't say a word; and about an hour later. he told George he didn't feel good.

He went home and about four days later he came back. George told him he sure hoped he didn't drink any of that bottle he took home,

George told him he had found the bottle and put brake fluid in., He said "No wonder I was in the bathroom so much." Then he got his tools and went home. I is a wonder it didn't kill him.

CHAPTER 67

"I DON'T CARE WHAT IT LOOKS LIKE"

Back in those days you had to burn the cars, but first you had to get all the seats and interior out, and pull the gas tanks off. Now days, you can leave seats and interior in them, and just split the gas tank, and you are ready to crush.

One night Randy was working the crane and George was guiding the cars when the chain came loose and hit George. It knocked him about twenty foot flat on his back, and cut his forehead. Randy took him to Dr. Couland's office while I w went to lock up. When I got to the doctor's office, I heard George say "take the big stitches. I don't care what it looks like. He was something else. I just loved that man.

CHAPTER 68
WINDOW PROBLEMS

Some time after George passed away, I called Mother one night and asked her if she wanted to go to Kmart with me. I was lonely, with nothing else to do. It was cold, but she said sure.. We went, but I didn't get a thing. Mother got one or two things. We left Kmart, went, and got us a coke, and started home. I said I wanted to wash the car, so I pulled into the car wash, rolled my window down to put the money in the machine, drove into the wash rack, but could not get my window up at all.

I told Mother it was goin' to hit us hard, about that time it was there. I let the ting get to the back of the car then put it in gear and got out of there. I finally got the window up, ran back into the wash rack and got a rinse. We was wet as we could be and cold,, but boy what a night.

CHAPTER 69

LEFT BEHIND, BUT NOT ALONE

We lost my daddy in 1988, I thought the world would stop, but I made through will the Lord's help. George was already sick with his lung cancer, and then in 1990 we lost him. We had been married 38 years..

But there was more. I lost my mother in 2010, the same year I came down with breast cancer.. I prayed and prayed, telling the Lord if I could only touch the hem of his garment, I'd be made whole. I took 38 treatments of radiation and they started me on the chemo tablet. I never gave up. I got up to 182 lbs. and was doing great; then two years ago I lost my sister. I had a little stroke, but still not giving up. God is on my side all the way.

My great grandson Dylan Duke has help me in lots of ways. also, my great granddaughter Paige Horton if I need to order anything she is always there to do for me.

CHAPTER 70

KEEPING BUSY WITH LIFE ALL AROUND ME

I Love to work with my hands. I still do wood work, crochet, knit embroider, and sew on the machine. I can't stand long because of my legs and back. I clean a little and sit a lot.

In 1996 I started taking care of foster kids. I had a monkey they all enjoyed very much. I loved fostering. I had good ones, and I had a few bad. I housed 113 up until 2010 when I came down with cancer, and mother was so sick. I could not handle it all, so I closed my home.

Randi my granddaughter married a trooper, Justin Pope My daughter Georgie married Mike Wegrzyn, another trooper. Now, granddaughter Shandy and my grandson Justin are both light horse police , I have been around law enforcement for a long time. They all called me Thad because they could not say Thaddues. I would laugh, I just laughed; it was my daddy's fault. He named me.

George bought me an old wood cook stove about 35 years ago, and we built a special room for it. We called it our antique room. I have things in there I would not take nothing for: Lauren's floor light m grandpa and grandma used in their store, a wind up record player that was my grandpa and grandma's, stand up milk separator I used when I was a kid, house harness we used with the horses, a water bucket and dipper, an old wash pan, an old style cabinet, Georgie's dad's chair that came all the way in covered wagon from Missouri, and an old cranking wrench daddy used on our old car. That is just a few things I have in there. In the winter on the weekends, we would cook breakfast out there set and watch the birds. If snow was on the ground there was more birds to watch, so we sat and drank our coffee we had boiled in the old time coffee pot,

I loved those days.

My grandpa and grandma came here in covered wagon. there was no roads. A group of wagons came together late of evening. They would all unhook the teams from their wagons. The men would go gather wood for fire and the women cooked supper.

They would make a circle with all the wagons, and Grandma said that after supper they would sit around the fire. Some would make music for a couple of hours, then they all went to their wagons to go to sleep. I have a trunk they carried in that wagon. I was just a little girl, but I loved for them to tell the story about their journey to Oklahoma. They landed in Ada and stayed in Ada. There was only one grocery store here.

My daddy was born here in Ada 1903, the baby of the family six older than him.

Well, here is 2021. I have had lots of good years.

God has been with me. I lost my dad, my mother, and my husband, plus a lot of other family members over the years, but God has carried me through it all. I still have my three children, my grandkids, great grandkids and even my great-great grandkids.

I am still in good shape and I am not alone. My God is still here with me.

I hope you enjoyed my book; and if you don't know God, I ask you to find a church and get to know him as I do, and you will be blessed.

CPSIA information can be obtained
at www.ICGtesting.com
Printed in the USA
BVHW031400250722
642942BV00014B/315